EUROPE IN 1360

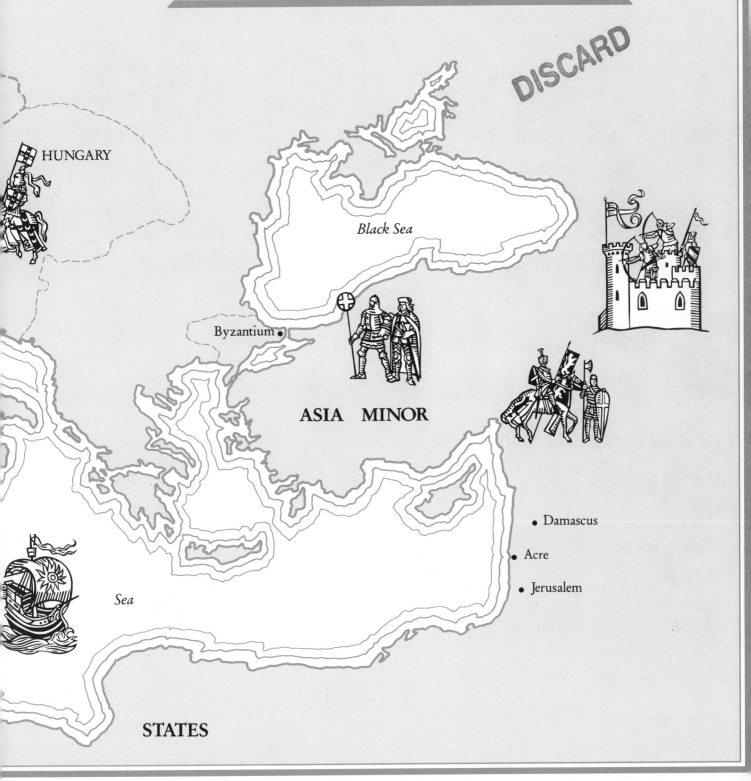

HUNGARY

Black Sea

Byzantium •

ASIA   MINOR

• Damascus

• Acre

• Jerusalem

Sea

STATES

KNIGHTS
IN ARMOR

LIVING HISTORY

KNIGHTS
IN ARMOR

JOHN D. CLARE, Editor

GULLIVER BOOKS
HARCOURT BRACE & COMPANY
SAN DIEGO   NEW YORK   LONDON

First U.S. edition 1992

First published in Great Britain in 1991 by The Bodley Head
Children's Books, an imprint of The Random Century Group Ltd
Created by Roxby Paintbox Co. Ltd

Gulliver Books is a registered trademark
of Harcourt Brace & Company.

Library of Congress Cataloging-in-Publication Data
Knights in armor/edited by John Clare.
p.   cm. — (Living history)
"Gulliver Books."
Summary: An overview of the lifestyle and changing role of the
knight during the Middle Ages.
ISBN 0-15-200508-0
ISBN 0-15-201308-3 (pbk.)
1. Knights and knighthood — Juvenile literature. 2. Civilization,
Medieval — Juvenile literature. [1. Knights and knighthood.
2. Civilization, Medieval.] I. Title. II. Series: Living history
(San Diego, Calif.)
CR4513.C58   1992
940.1 — dc20   91-2766

Director of Photography   Tymn Lyntell
Photography   Charles Best
Art Director   Dalia Hartman
Production Manager   Fiona Nicholson
Visualization/Systems Operator   Antony Parks
Typesetting   Thompson Type, San Diego, California
Reproduction   F. E. Burman Ltd
                 Columbia Offset Ltd
                 Dalim Computer Graphic Systems U.K. Ltd
                 J. Film Process Ltd
                 Trademasters Ltd

Printed and bound in China

B C D E
A B C D E (pbk.)

ACKNOWLEDGMENTS

Advisor: Richard Fletcher, University of York. **Costumes:** Val
Metheringham, Joanna Measure. **Makeup:** Alex Cawdron, Louise
Fisher, Caroline Kelly, Sarah Packham, Jan Harrison Shell. **Models:**
Chris Lovell, Neville Smith. **Props:** Caroline Gardener, Mark Roberts.
Period consultant, fight director, and **casting:** Mike Loades assisted
by Gordon Summers. **Photographer's assistant:** Alex Rhodes. **Picture
research:** Valerie Tongue.

Additional photographs: Reproduced by courtesy of the Trustees of the
British Museum, p. 63 top left; Glasgow University Library, p. 62 left;
Michael Boys/Susan Griggs Agency, pp. 58–59; Antony Parks,
pp. 24–25, 28–29, 34–35; Public Record Office, p. 62 right (DL 10/38);
Ronald Sheridan's Photo-Library, p. 6 top and bottom; Zefa Picture
Library, pp. 26–27, 44–45, 56–57.

Contents

The Coming of the Knights

The "Age of the Knight" began in about A.D. 900 and lasted until around 1500, the end of the period historians call the Middle Ages. This was a time of great contrasts — of warriors and saints, kings and serfs, and pageantry and splendor alongside famine, epidemics, and overwhelming poverty.

Most of Europe was divided into small states, each ruled by a duke or a count who was supposed to obey his king or emperor, but in practice often did as he pleased. One state was ruled by the Pope.

Viking raids in the 9th century had nearly destroyed the Church. A Council of Bishops held near Soissons in A.D. 909 complained that the abbeys had been demolished and Christian customs forgotten. During the Middle Ages, however, the Catholic Church regained its power. Many new monasteries were built and a strict regime was imposed on the monks. The Church developed canon law (rules laying down what a Christian had to believe) and a court system called the Inquisition to find and punish heretics (people who disagreed with Church teachings). In the Middle Ages you would be denounced as a heretic if you believed that the earth traveled around the sun or doubted the story of creation in the Bible. Science was dominated by the ideas of ancient writers such as the Greeks, and most people were Roman Catholics and accepted the Pope as their spiritual leader.

THE DIVISIONS OF SOCIETY

Medieval society was divided into three groups: the clergy, the workers, and the warriors. Children of wealthier families often became knights or entered the

Church if they did not inherit land. But the majority of people were workers and most of these were villeins (peasants), who worked in the fields. Peasants were very poor. Large families commonly lived to-

gether in one-room huts that they shared with farm animals.

The rest of the workers, who engaged in crafts or trade, lived in the towns. There were few large towns in the Middle Ages; only a dozen in the whole of Europe had over 100,000 inhabitants. The Church said that towns were "accursed" places. Church leaders forbade moneylending or trading for profit and condemned many trades as "contemptible professions" because, they said, such trades encouraged the seven deadly sins. Merchants and cooks were greedy; innkeepers and cloth-makers encouraged lust. Other tradesmen condemned by the Church included doctors, gardeners, pastry-makers, cobblers, and tripe-sellers. Even beggars were criticized — they were guilty of laziness.

Nonetheless, as the Middle Ages continued, towns and trade expanded. Italian towns such as Venice began to trade with the Middle East, Persia, and India. Marco Polo traveled to China. Craftspeople banded together in groups called guilds to control their industry and maintain standards. The none (noon) bell was changed from its original time of 2:00 P.M. to 12:00 noon, perhaps to reduce the workers' lunchtime. Some workers tried to strike, but they were told that the working day was "from the hour of sunrise to the hour of sunset."

Life was short and difficult: most people never reached 30. Frequent wars, famines, and epidemics such as the Black Death killed many people. Even entertainment could be brutal. The wealthy hunted and jousted, while the poor wrestled or fought with staves. People enjoyed such bloody spectacles as blind beggars vying to beat a pig to death and accidentally hitting each other. City authorities built stages in the marketplaces, where criminals were publicly tortured. Undeterred, bands of outlaws roamed unsettled areas.

THE WARRIOR CLASS

The main roles of the knight were to fight wars and protect the interests of the landed classes both at home and abroad. Knights did not necessarily help relations between Europe and its neighbors to the south and east, though. The wars of the Middle Ages often harmed trade, and contacts with Muslim Africa and the East became more and more difficult.

Within Europe, particularly in the early Middle Ages, knights were sometimes dangerous and difficult to control. In the 11th century, the Church declared the Truce of God to restrain them from harming clergy and peasants. Protecting the poor and helpless became part of a code of behavior called chivalry. Chivalrous knights were to be gallant and brave, gentle and bold, pure and pious.

The word "chivalry" comes from the French word *chevalier* or "horseman." At first the knight was simply a cavalry soldier who had promised to serve a ruler in exchange for a share of land. Because knights supplied their own war-horses and armor, rulers had to give them enough land so that they could afford to equip themselves. With their land, the knights acquired legal and governmental duties that gave them power and social standing. As the status of the knight changed, wealthy men wanted to be knighted. Even kings had their sons knighted.

The Development of Armor

Scholars once believed that the Middle Ages produced few advances in knowledge or technology, but in warfare there were many discoveries. As new weapons were invented, new armor was developed.

In the 11th and 12th centuries, knights wore hauberks (coats of mail). The most common sort of mail was made from interlocking metal rings. Another kind, called scale armor, was made from small pieces of metal riveted to a leather tunic. Beneath the hauberk, knights wore a padded jacket, called an acton or gambeson, to help cushion blows and prevent the metal from chafing. Mail armor, which weighed about 30 pounds (13.5 kilograms), became unbearably hot in direct sunlight. To deflect the sun's rays and to prevent the armor from rusting, knights usually put a surcoat (light tunic) over their hauberks.

During the 13th and 14th centuries, knights started wearing steel plate extensions to protect more vulnerable parts of their bodies. They covered their heads with great metal *topfhelms* (pot helmets). The foot soldiers of the time said that the only way to kill a knight was to knock him to the ground and beat him to death.

Left: A 12th-century knight wears mail armor. The mail mittens, called mufflers, have leather palms to protect his hands. Mail chausses (trousers) protect his legs and feet; a mail coif protects his shoulders. A red acton (padded jacket) shows through beneath his surcoat. The knight's helm bears his heraldic crest.
Center: By the 14th century, plate covers the vulnerable parts of a knight's body. Pauldrons, couters, gauntlets, cuisses, and poleyns cover the shoulders, elbows, hands, thighs, and knees. The knight still wears a mail skirt and a mail collar attached to a bascinet (helmet) with a hounskull (pig-faced) visor that can be raised for a breath of air.
Right: By the late 15th century, plate armor has been perfected, and the knight can be completely covered.

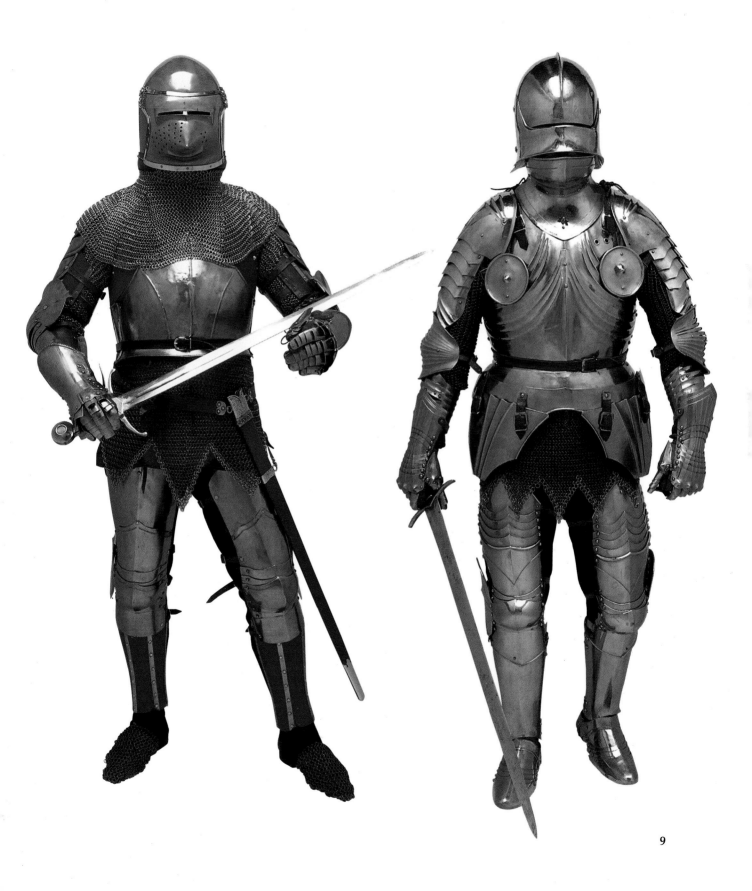

The Royal Progress

At his coronation, a medieval king received a sword and a crown — symbols of his power and authority. Priests anointed him with holy oil and proclaimed him "king by the grace of God."

The king had to defend the country, make laws, and enforce them with terrible punishments. His power even extended to healing the sick. Scrofula was called the king's evil because a king's touch was supposed to cure it. If a king was too weak, his subjects would rebel.

Protected by his knights, a king traveled around the kingdom making sure that the nobles and judges were upholding his laws. His royal court of chamberlains, stewards, treasurers, clerks, and chaplains accompanied him, although in the early Middle Ages the king's wife and the wives of his knights did not.

Henry II of England (1154–89) "was always on the move, traveling in unbearably long stages, and in this respect merciless beyond measure to the household that accompanied him." Even when exhausted, he would decide to move on in the middle of the night. "Immediately everywhere is confusion," wrote one eyewitness. "Men run about like mad, wagons crash into each other, and packhorses are quickly loaded."

Following just behind the main court are dozens of servants: cooks, butlers, grooms, valets, jesters, and washerwomen. With them travel disgruntled subjects who wish to bring their legal cases directly to the king.

Accidents are common on the poorly maintained roads. These women call for help to right the cart; they don't want to be left behind, because stragglers frequently fall prey to outlaws, robbers, and murderers.

The Feudal System

Kings did not directly finance a cavalry. A knight's horses and armor were very costly. Instead of paying knights wages, a medieval king granted fiefs, or estates, to a number of men from powerful families. In return, these men, called barons, promised to provide a certain number of knights during times of trouble when the king would proclaim the *arrière-ban* (call to arms). In England in 1205 the cavalry comprised about 5,000 knights.

Some kings demanded more than knights from their barons. Henry de la Wade supplied his king with falcons in return for 520 acres. Rowland le Sarcere held 110 acres on the condition that every Christmas he would come before the king and perform "a jump, a puff, and a rude noise."

Like kings, the barons granted the use of land to tenants who supplied them with goods or services in return. Barons granted manors to knights who promised to fight for them. A blacksmith might get four acres and a smithy in return for shoeing the baron's horses and mending the plows.

Any man who had been granted land was called a vassal and had to swear allegiance to his lord. Kneeling down, he placed both hands between those of the lord and said, "I become your man from this day forward, and unto you shall be true and faithful for the lands I hold from you."

This villein, or peasant, is hoeing a field, preparing it for cultivation. Her family has been granted the use of a small plot of land by the local lord. In return, they must work for the lord or give him a portion of their produce. A successful harvest is vital for everyone, including the lord. If the village fields do not produce enough food, many people will starve.

The villeins' lives are full of hard work. In addition to working the fields, they protect and care for livestock (above, top), cultivate new land, and work in the vineyards and gardens of the lord (above).

In the Pillory

When a knight was granted land by the king or a baron, the villeins, who were bound to the land, became his property as part of his fief. As lord of the manor, a knight was entitled to receive goods and services from the villeins who lived on the estate. In one typical village, each family of villeins held 30 acres of land, which they were allowed to farm. In return, they had to work on the lord's land two days a week, put in extra hours at harvest time, guard the castle, and wait on the lord's table at Christmas. Every year, each family gave the lord 48 bags of malt, 16 bags of grain, 8 cartloads of wood, 30 hens, and 1,000 eggs.

A villein was also required to pay special taxes when he took up a tenancy or if his daughter married. When a villein died, his family paid the lord a heriot of the best animal and sometimes all the furniture. These heavy taxes left little for the villeins. If the lord failed to exercise his rights, however, the villeins became the owners of the land.

Sometimes humiliating services were added to a villein's many duties. In one

French village, the peasants had to kiss the door of the manor house. In another, they had to stay up all night beating the moat of the lord's castle to prevent the frogs from croaking and disturbing his lady. In many villages, the lord could stay with a villein's daughter on her wedding night.

At regular intervals the lord of the manor held a court baron, or manor court, to settle grievances and control his tenants. At the court, villagers would be given punishments for such infractions as chopping down the lord's trees, grazing cattle on his land, or attacking their neighbors.

Some knights inflicted punishments where there had been no crimes. They plundered villages and tortured peasants, crushing them in narrow chests lined with nails and sharp stones. They thought that "villeins, like trees, grow better if they are cut back."

This villein is a troublesome man who is brought before the manor court nearly every year. This time he has seized a pig and attacked the bailiff who looks after the lord's property. He is locked all day in the pillory, where the villagers hurl abuse at him and bombard him with vegetables and stones.

Paying Tithes

In the Middle Ages, the Church dominated the lives of everyone — from kings to villeins. Because land was generally inherited by the eldest son, the younger sons of noble families often entered the priesthood. Like the lord of the manor, priests collected taxes, called tithes, from the villagers.

People believed that if they were wicked "the devils would seize them and carry them away to hell" when they died. Even good people expected to spend thousands of years in purgatory before going to heaven.

The Church claimed the power to hasten the way to heaven by granting indulgences that reduced time in purgatory, or to doom people to hell by excommunicating them and refusing Christian burial. In 1076 when Pope Gregory VII excommunicated the Holy Roman Emperor Henry IV, the king crossed the snow-covered Alps in midwinter to beg the Pope's forgiveness.

The Church exerted its influence over knights as well as kings. In 1041 a Church council in France proclaimed the Truce of

God. The council forbade soldiers to fight on Sundays or holy days and declared that the proper tasks of a knight were to defend the Church and the poor, and to fight against evil.

A monk collects the tithes (tenths) from the villagers. He demands a tenth of everything — crops, fruit, hay, livestock, and milk. Merchants and craftsmen pay a tenth of their profits.

People often resent paying the tithe to the priest, who can keep it all for himself and live in luxury. Some farmers take the milk tithe to the church in large buckets. If they find no one present, they pour the milk on the floor in front of the altar.

Pilgrimage

One way to do penance in the Middle Ages was to visit the shrine of a dead saint. These journeys were called pilgrimages. Often knights went on a pilgrimage to atone for the violence of their lives. Fulk the Black, a French count who had massacred his enemies and murdered his wife, made three pilgrimages to Jerusalem. There he had monks beat him with branches as he shouted, "Accept, O Lord, the wretched Fulk."

Ordinary people went on pilgrimages hoping to be healed at a holy place or simply to see the sights. In Rome, a pilgrim might see an altar built by St. Peter, a self-portrait of the Virgin Mary, the table used for the Last Supper, and the napkin that had covered the face of Jesus. People who had visited Rome wore a small napkin as a badge and were called Romers. Compostela pilgrims wore a seashell from the local beach, and people who had been to Jerusalem were called Palmers for the palm leaf that they wore.

Pilgrims, like those in Chaucer's *Canterbury Tales*, sometimes traveled in groups along with thieves and murderers who had been ordered to go on a pilgrimage instead of going to prison. They carried travel guides telling them what to take and where to stay.

A group of knights formed the society of the Knights Templar in 1118 to protect pilgrims on their way to the Holy Land. Pilgrims could deposit money at Templar castles in the West and withdraw it when they reached Jerusalem. The Templars even arranged transportation, accommodation, and guarded trips to places of interest.

These pilgrims are traveling along the busiest road in Europe on their way to the shrine of St. James of Compostela in Spain. Here they pause at a small roadside shrine set up to attract passersby.

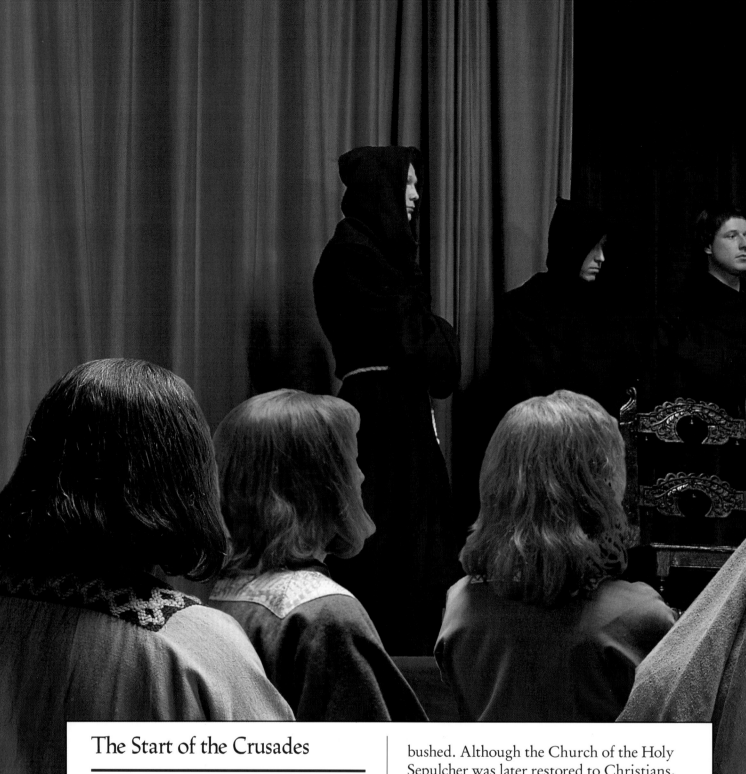

The Start of the Crusades

Since A.D. 638 Jerusalem had been controlled by local Muslim rulers. In 1009 the Muslims destroyed the Church of the Holy Sepulcher, Christ's tomb in Jerusalem, and began a series of attacks on Christian pilgrims. Hundreds were killed in 1064 when a party of 12,000 pilgrims was ambushed. Although the Church of the Holy Sepulcher was later restored to Christians, many Europeans wanted Jerusalem to be recaptured by a Christian army.

There were other pressures for a military crusade. The younger sons of noblemen hoped to win wealth and glory. The Roman Catholic Church thought a holy war would keep the violent knights usefully occupied. And the Church was having troubles of its

own. When Urban II became Pope in 1088, the Church was divided: two men claimed to be Pope. Urban II hoped a crusade would help him gain an advantage over his rival. Some people believed that signs proved God wanted a crusade. Stars had fallen from heaven and children had been born with extra limbs. One priest insisted that he had seen a crusader and a Saracen (Muslim) fighting in the air.

At the end of the 11th century, Muslim armies attacked the Byzantine Empire. When the emperor sent to Italy for help, Urban II called for a crusade.

It is November 27, 1095. Pope Urban II has summoned France's leading churchmen to Clermont. Jerusalem, he tells them, is held by God's enemies, and he lists Muslim atrocities. "Who will avenge all this? Who will repair the damage?" he cries. "God wills that we should do it!" shout the people. They will spread the idea of a holy war.

The First Crusade

In 1095 Urban II traveled around Europe for eight months encouraging people to go on a crusade to free the Holy Land. In Germany, thousands of peasants became so enthusiastic that they set off immediately. They were led by Peter the Hermit, a preacher, and Walter the Penniless, a poor knight. They fought their way through Hungary, looting and burning as they went. When they reached Asia Minor (now part of Turkey), they confronted the Muslims but were quickly destroyed.

Several months later about 4,000 knights and 26,000 foot soldiers set out from Byzantium. After a three-year campaign they captured Jerusalem on July 15, 1099. According to one witness, they slaughtered the Muslims until they "waded in blood up to their ankles," then they seized all the gold, silver, and horses to be found in the city. Finally, they went to worship at Christ's tomb.

Some knights fought for wealth and glory. Others were more religious. They joined orders of chivalry such as the Templars or the Hospitallers and promised to live in poverty and to remain unmarried.

They frowned on worldly pastimes such as feasting, singing, and chess. One Templar, nicknamed Sir Bread-and-Water, was so weakened from fasting that he fell from his horse whenever he was hit in battle.

Although some wealthy crusaders travel in comfort with their entire households, this poor French knight takes only his squire and the most basic equipment, weapons, and clothing (inset). He leaves his wife to manage the tiny fief with the help of a few old servants.

Before setting off, he has confessed his sins, taken Communion, and received the Church's blessing. Now he goes "to break heads and arms, to hear the cries of 'At them,' to kill the heathen," and, perhaps, to win his fortune.

The Defeat of the Crusades

Duuring the next 200 years, six more crusades were launched to defend the Kingdom of Jerusalem established in 1099.

The conflict was bitter and vicious. When the army of the Second Crusade marched on Damascus in 1148, the Muslims attacked them in an orchard. The crusaders built stockades, but the Muslims stabbed them through the walls. Christians on the Third Crusade ate the flesh of murdered Muslim hostages, and Richard the Lionheart hung Saracens' (Muslims') heads from his saddle. After the capture of one town, the crusaders executed 2,700 prisoners, then ripped open the corpses to find jewels that might have been swallowed.

The crusaders' desire for glory often brought military disaster. At the Battle of Cresson (1187) the Templars' Grand Master

taunted a band of knights until they attacked the main Muslim army. Only three knights survived. The Kingdom of Jerusalem, with 1,500 knights at most, lost 100 men in this one foolish charge.

Many crusaders quarreled, plotted against each other, and were more interested in plunder than battle. Instead of attacking the Muslims, the Fourth Crusade looted Byzantium, a city they were supposed to be defending. The crusaders were too few in number and too far from Europe to resist the Muslim armies forever. In 1244, Muslims retook Jerusalem. The last crusader stronghold in the Holy Land, the city of Acre, fell 47 years later. This loss ended the Christian Kingdom of Jerusalem.

When unable to defeat the heavily armed crusaders in direct confrontation, Muslim soldiers mount surprise attacks on supply convoys and stragglers. Here, a party of lightly armed horsemen ambushes a scouting party of crusaders.

A Woman's Role

Although women were considered subordinate to men of their rank, they established their own place in the Church and on the manor. Some even became involved in war and politics. Eleanor of Aquitaine went on crusade in full armor. She divorced King Louis VII of France and married the future Henry II of England, against whom she later led a rebellion.

Typically, a knight's wife organized domestic tasks such as cooking, brewing, making clothes, and picking lice out of everyone's hair. She hired laborers, supervised stewards, sold produce, and kept accounts. She also, when necessary, organized the defense of the castle. The Countess of Buchan defended Berwick Castle so fiercely against King Edward I of England that, when he finally overcame her soldiers, he hung her over the battlements in an iron cage. In 1341 the Countess of Brittany defended her husband's castle and led a counterattack with what one writer called "the courage of a man and the bravery of a lion."

Women could become honorary members of certain knightly orders, such as the Order of St. John of Jerusalem. They were known as Chevalieres. In France, an Order of Cordeliers was created solely for widows.

In the violent world of the Middle Ages, men often died before their wives. The widow of a nobleman often managed an estate in her own right or on behalf of a young son. Christine de Pisan, widowed at 25, supported her family by writing.

Expecting attack while her husband is away, a noblewoman directs the construction of hoardings from which missiles and boiling oil can be dropped.

Women in the Solar

Women had many responsibilities, and a few were famous and powerful, but they were not regarded as men's equals in the Middle Ages. Church leaders argued that women were evil. Had not Eve eaten the apple and caused Adam to sin? "Woman," wrote one churchman, "is of feeble kind, and makes more lies."

Although the Virgin Mary was revered, many believed that the four sayings recorded in the Bible were *all* that Mary had said in her entire life. Medieval ladies were advised to follow Mary's example, to keep quiet and to devote themselves to their domestic jobs — "like slaves or prisoners," complained one wife.

In wealthy families, marriage was used to secure social and political advantage.

Gracia, daughter of Thomas de Sakeby, an English noble, was married in 1198 to Adam de Neville. She was 4 years old. Before she was 11, she had been widowed twice and married again. In 1449, 20-year-old Elizabeth Paston was beaten by her mother as often as twice a day for over three months because she refused to marry a widower of 50 who had been permanently disfigured by illness.

A girl was taught to obey her husband. The law let a man beat his wife if he thought she was at fault, even for such presumed offenses as giving birth to a mentally handicapped child.

The lord's wife and her ladies-in-waiting have retired to the solar — the ladies' room. This is their exclusive world, where they cultivate a refined society. They embroider, weave cloth, play chess, make music, and read stories of love and chivalry. Men are only admitted if they can prove that they are educated, polite, and witty.

Pages and Squires

When a boy was born into a noble household, news of the birth was rushed to the father. The bearer of such good news was richly rewarded. Because mothers were often too young to look after their babies themselves — many wives gave birth in their early teens — a nurse of the appropriate rank was hired.

Boys' games taught them how to behave like knights. One game was called "robber baron," and another, "the king doesn't lie." Boys made hobbyhorses and showed off for girls by charging at each other.

At seven, the son of a knight became a page in another nobleman's household. He spent the next seven years learning to ride, to hunt, to handle hawks, to play chess and music, to dance, and to behave properly. "Do not scratch your head, nor spit too far. . . . Do not sigh, or belch, or with

puffing and blowing cast foul breath upon your lord," advised the 14th-century *Babees Book*. The page served at table to learn that the highest honor was to serve others. He was taught to love God and to be devoted to a lady. A woman in the household would become the page's special friend so he could learn how to treat a lady.

At 14, the page became a squire. In a short church ceremony, the squire was blessed by a priest and girded with a sword and baldric (belt). For the next seven years he trained for battle and the joust. He still served at meals, but now he performed the more important tasks of pouring the wine or carving the meat. The squire of honor stood by his lord's chair, carried his helmet and banner, led his horse, and raised his battle cry.

A page and a squire serve at table (left). Squires (main picture) fight with staves, hawk, practice archery, and learn to charge using a quintain as a target. A highborn squire plays the rebec (below).

The Accolade

By the age of 21, a squire had completed his training, but he did not automatically become a knight. Those who were too poor to buy their own equipment might remain squires all their lives. A rich nobleman's son, on the other hand, might be knighted when he was only 12 years old. A knight was a soldier in the army, but knighthood was also a grade of society and wealthy people did not want their sons to remain mere squires.

People believed that knighthood was a holy calling. The knighting ceremony, called the accolade, was a religious occasion. On the evening before the ceremony, the young squire was given a bath, symbolizing the washing away of his sins. He lay on a bed to dry, to remind him of the rest that God would give brave knights in heaven. In the morning, dressed in a white shirt, a gold tunic, and a purple cloak, he was dubbed by the king.

In the late Middle Ages, the knighting ceremony was very elaborate. A priest blessed the young man's sword. Then the squire vowed to obey the rules of chivalry and never to run away in battle. The king dubbed him by delivering a blow on the neck with the flat of his sword. Finally ladies buckled on his armor, starting with the spurs — the symbol of courage.

To give them courage, squires might also be knighted before a battle. Once, the Earl of Suffolk knighted a soldier who had captured him — he was too proud to allow himself to be captured by a mere squire.

This squire has won his spurs by showing courage in battle. On the field, the ceremony is brief. The lord simply hits the man hard on his shoulder and says, "Be thou a knight." The blow, with the sword or the hand, is called the accolade.

Knight Errantry

During the 12th century two kinds of heroic stories became popular. One, the *chansons de geste*, were songs about the deeds of the great Emperor Charlemagne. The other, romances, were stories of King Arthur, a legendary 6th-century king who ruled England with his Knights of the Round Table. In the romances, the heroes were knights errant who rode out to fight dragons, rescue damsels, and find the Holy Grail (the cup used at the Last Supper).

Many medieval knights heard these stories and decided that they, too, would become knights errant. They asked ladies in the court for scarves or gloves to wear as marks of special favor. Then they put green tunics over their armor and green covers over their shields and traveled around Europe fighting for good causes.

Other knights traveled to support themselves. A knight needed at least three horses, armor, and the services of a squire, all of which were expensive. In addition society expected a knight to be generous, even extravagant — one 12th-century knight sowed a field with 30,000 silver coins. Knights might try to make a living from prize money at tournaments. Successful knights were the popular heroes of their day. The 13th-century jouster Ulrich von Lichtenstein toured Italy, Austria, and Germany. He dressed as Venus, the Roman goddess of love, and promised to give all his horses to any knight who defeated him. Those he defeated had to bow down in honor of Ulrich's lady.

A knight passes through a village on the way to the next tournament. His squire follows with the booty the knight won in his last melee (a fight between teams of knights), when he captured and ransomed a number of wealthy knights.

Chivalry

In 1265 a Spanish knight, Raimon Llull, wrote that knights must be chivalrous — truthful, kind to the poor, loyal, and courteous — even in war.

The Law of Arms laid down how knights had to behave in battle. They could not mistreat captives or leave an enemy knight to die of his wounds. At the Battle of Poitiers (1356), King Jean II of France postponed his attack to avoid fighting on a Sunday. The delay, which allowed the English time to prepare, cost him the victory.

During the 12th century some knights became troubadours. They sang songs of chivalry and love. Influenced by these songs, many knights gave their hearts to young ladies. It did not matter if the lady was married; in the Middle Ages marriage was often a business arrangement, and a knight believed true love was the hopeless longing for someone you could never marry.

This courtly love was one of the strangest aspects of chivalry. Knights performed great feats just to win a smile. One knight fought in a tournament wearing his lady's dress instead of his armor. He was badly wounded. The lady's husband gave a feast in the knight's honor, and the lady wore the bloodstained dress. Harsh words were exchanged before the Battle of Poitiers when Sir John Chandos and Sir Jean de Clermont discovered they were wearing the favor of the same woman.

In 1186 the writer Andreas Capellanus listed 31 laws of love. In 1400 the ladies of France, led by the poet Christine de Pisan, set up a Court of Love. It heard cases such as that against a lady who had asked a knight to wear her favor but then had not attended the tournament.

A lady ties her scarf to her knight's arm, and he vows to fight for her in the tournament. The motto on her tent reads, Jealousy Is the Enemy of Honor.

Making Armor

B y the 14th century, armor was made to fit each knight individually. A team of craftsmen worked on the armor — hammerers; mail makers; millmen, who polished the metal; locksmiths, who attached the hinges; and engravers and etchers, who decorated it with designs and inscriptions intended to give a knight spiritual protection.

The best armorers were from Germany and northern Italy, but their armor was sold

all over Europe. Armorers stamped their family emblem on the steel to show who had made it. In the 15th century, Petrajolo Missaglia of Milan sometimes added an appropriate quotation from the Bible, such as "Jesus passed safely through the crowd." Less skilled smiths from local villages forged Petrajolo's mark and sold their imitations as genuine Missaglia armor.

Well-made armor was almost indestructible. It might get battered and dented, but it could be hammered out. Every army took a portable forge for making repairs. During one tournament, friends of the English knight William Marshal found him lying with his head on a blacksmith's anvil while the smith hammered at it — a heavy blow had trapped his head inside his helmet.

A nobleman examines the plate armor he is having made, while a hammerer beats out the plates from billets of steel forged in the smithy, and a master armorer beats a helmet into shape (below).

A mail maker (below far right and inset left) rivets circlets of wire together into interlocking rings. He follows a pattern, counting the rings in the same way a knitter counts stitches. In each completed suit he inserts a single ring of brass stamped with his name.

Arming the Knight

I t took an hour for a squire, sometimes assisted by a servant, to help a knight into a suit of plate armor. Beneath his armor, the knight wore a padded doublet lined with satin and a pair of worsted pants called hose. Strips of blanket around his knees kept the armor from rubbing.

First, the squire puts the sabatons (mail shoes) on the knight and clips the greaves around his calves. Then he buckles the cuisses onto the knight's upper leg with leather straps (above and inset right).

Next, the mail skirt is tied to the points, the laces that hang from the doublet (above and inset far right). Then come the padded backplate and breastplate, followed by the vambraces and gauntlets that protect the knight's arms and hands.

Finally, with the addition of his spurs, helmet, and jousting shield, the knight is armed from head to toe.

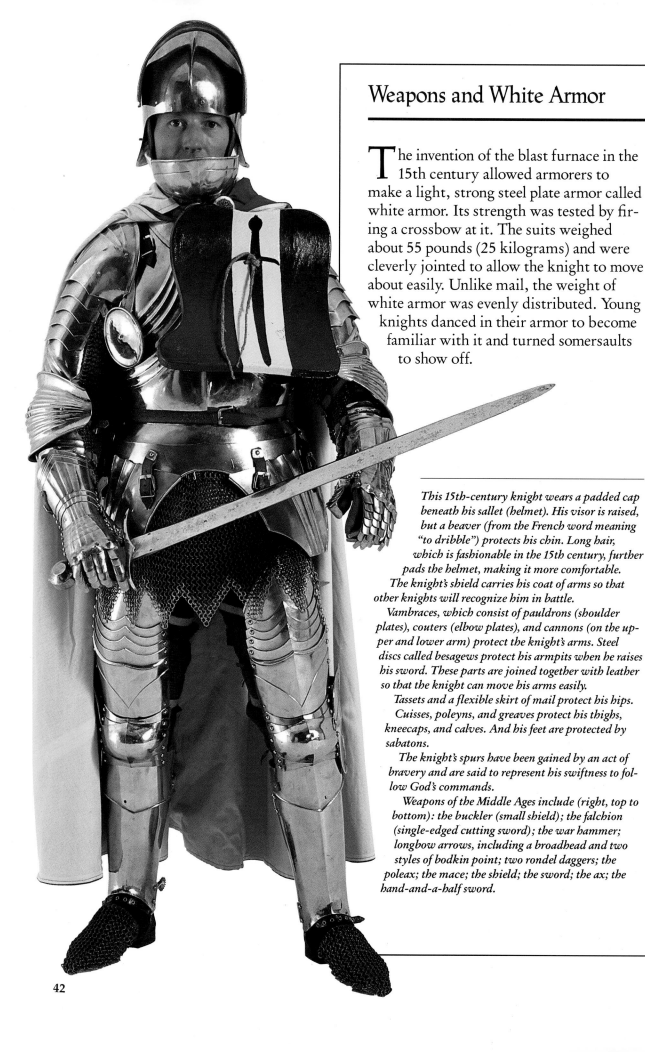

Weapons and White Armor

The invention of the blast furnace in the 15th century allowed armorers to make a light, strong steel plate armor called white armor. Its strength was tested by firing a crossbow at it. The suits weighed about 55 pounds (25 kilograms) and were cleverly jointed to allow the knight to move about easily. Unlike mail, the weight of white armor was evenly distributed. Young knights danced in their armor to become familiar with it and turned somersaults to show off.

This 15th-century knight wears a padded cap beneath his sallet (helmet). His visor is raised, but a beaver (from the French word meaning "to dribble") protects his chin. Long hair, which is fashionable in the 15th century, further pads the helmet, making it more comfortable.

The knight's shield carries his coat of arms so that other knights will recognize him in battle.

Vambraces, which consist of pauldrons (shoulder plates), couters (elbow plates), and cannons (on the upper and lower arm) protect the knight's arms. Steel discs called besagews protect his armpits when he raises his sword. These parts are joined together with leather so that the knight can move his arms easily.

Tassets and a flexible skirt of mail protect his hips.

Cuisses, poleyns, and greaves protect his thighs, kneecaps, and calves. And his feet are protected by sabatons.

The knight's spurs have been gained by an act of bravery and are said to represent his swiftness to follow God's commands.

Weapons of the Middle Ages include (right, top to bottom): the buckler (small shield); the falchion (single-edged cutting sword); the war hammer; longbow arrows, including a broadhead and two styles of bodkin point; two rondel daggers; the poleax; the mace; the shield; the sword; the ax; the hand-and-a-half sword.

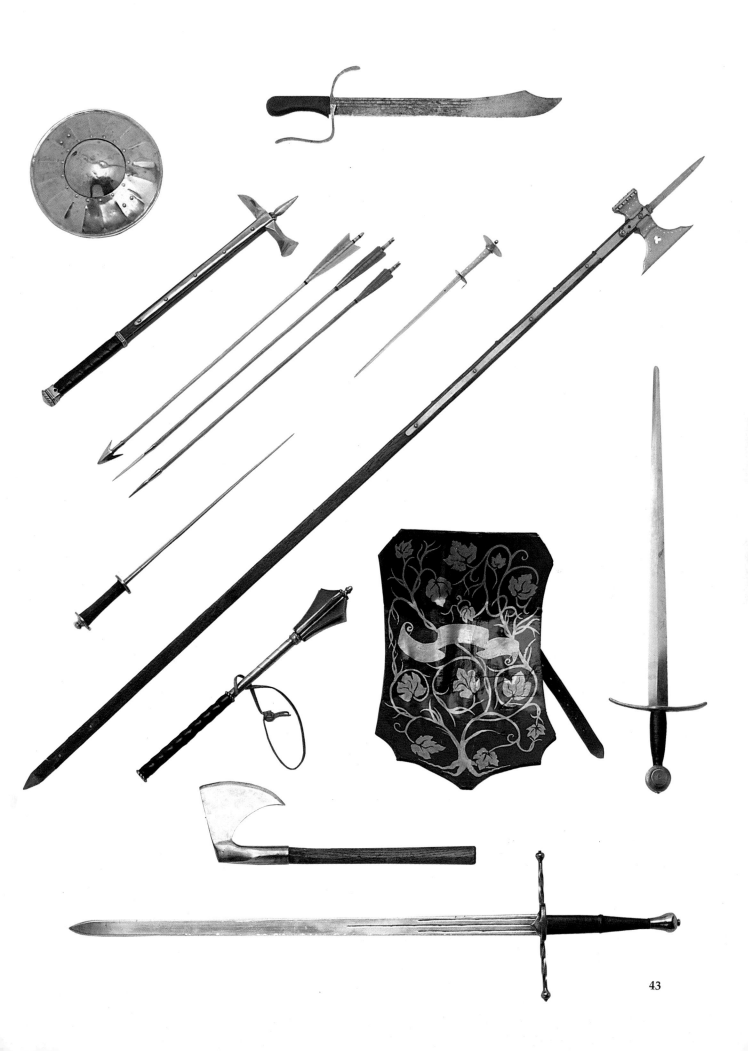

The Siege

A knight did not spend all his life fighting glorious battles. Even when he was away at war, much of his time was spent besieging castles or walled towns.

A siege was a long and costly affair, so an army usually tried to take a castle by surprise. More than one castle was captured when a soldier climbed up the sewage chute and lowered the drawbridge.

If surprise failed, the attackers would try to capture the castle by direct assault, using scaling ladders and belfries (siege towers). They pounded the walls with battering rams and hurled rocks weighing up to 300 pounds (136 kilograms) from machines called mangonels and trebuchets. They also threw dead horses and prisoners' heads over the castle walls to spread disease and alarm.

The defenders, however, still had the advantage. Castle design improved greatly during the Middle Ages and by the 15th century a large castle could be defended by as few as 60 men-at-arms and 180 archers. The archers fired upon the enemy from towers along the walls, while other soldiers poured boiling oil and Greek fire (burning naphtha or petroleum) from hoardings built out over the battlements.

The attacking army has decided to mine the castle, so sappers are digging a tunnel under the castle walls. When they have finished, they will burn the timber supports that prop up the tunnel roof. The unsupported tunnel will collapse, bringing down the section of wall above. As soon as this happens, the attackers will be able to fight their way into the castle through the gap in the defenses.

Within the castle walls, the soldiers build a barricade in the courtyard and wait to defend themselves against the assault.

Starving Out the Enemy

If all attempts at assault failed, the attacking army surrounded the town or castle and began to starve it out. Sometimes they built a rival castle called a malvoisin (bad neighbor) nearby. In the worst cases — such as at Rouen in 1419 — those trapped in the city became so hungry they ate dogs and rats and let their children starve.

Those under siege often expelled people unable to fight, but the attacking armies sometimes refused to let them leave. At Calais in 1346, 500 women and children, trapped between the English and French armies, starved to death.

Camping outside the walls, the attacking soldiers suffered from heat, flies, and dysentery. As many knights died from disease during sieges as from injuries in battles.

During a long siege, knights grew restless. They sometimes relieved their frustration by hanging prisoners in front of the castle walls. The inhabitants retaliated with surprise attacks. During a siege at Ploërmel in Brittany (1351), 30 English and 30 French knights fought a battle to the death. The survivors were the heroes of their day.

The exasperation of the siege explains why the fall of a castle or a town resulted in a massacre. At the start of a siege, a town was called on to surrender. If it refused, then according to custom, the besieging army had the right to kill all the inhabitants.

During a siege, tents are provided for heralds, minstrels, surgeons, and a host of workers, as well as for the thousands of soldiers. These 15th-century Burgundian knights are waiting for a battle to begin. Meanwhile, a servant makes a stew with ingredients pillaged from the local peasants.

Fighting on Horseback

A massed force of knights charging on horseback formed the elite corps of every medieval army. "The horse and lance," wrote Jean de Bueil, a 15th-century knight, "are the most dangerous weapons in the world. They are unstoppable."

Yet knights had few chances to fight in a major battle. Most campaigns aimed to damage the enemy's economy by destroying the countryside without becoming bogged down in a long siege. Scouts and incendi-aries attacked villages on foot, setting fire to the buildings. The role of the cavalry was simply to chase and cut down the fleeing villagers. In such warfare the knight, called "a terrible worm in an iron cocoon," by one eyewitness, was almost invincible.

Pitched battles in which opposing forces engaged in close combat were rare. Large armies were difficult to maneuver and, having drawn close, often wandered apart by accident. In most campaigns knights fought other knights only in minor con-flicts (called skirmishes) involving small numbers when hostile scouting parties

met by chance. Before the Battle of Poitiers in 1356, King Jean II of France had no idea where the English army was positioned, even though it was only a few miles away. He searched in entirely the wrong direction until the English scouts, against orders, attacked the French rear. Most battles were arranged; the commanders agreed to meet at a certain place at a certain time.

When finally given the chance to fight in a major battle, the knights were almost uncontrollable. The Frenchman Jean Froissart wrote that in the Hundred Years' War between England and France (1337–1453) "the commanders could not stop them from attacking; they were too eager." Knights fought grouped into disorderly units called *bannières*. At Poitiers the senior French knights insisted on riding in the first cavalry charge. Wallowing through the mud into a hail of arrows, the French lost all three of their military commanders in the opening moments of the battle.

Two hostile scouting parties clash in a small skirmish before a battle. The knights deliver huge swinging blows with their swords.

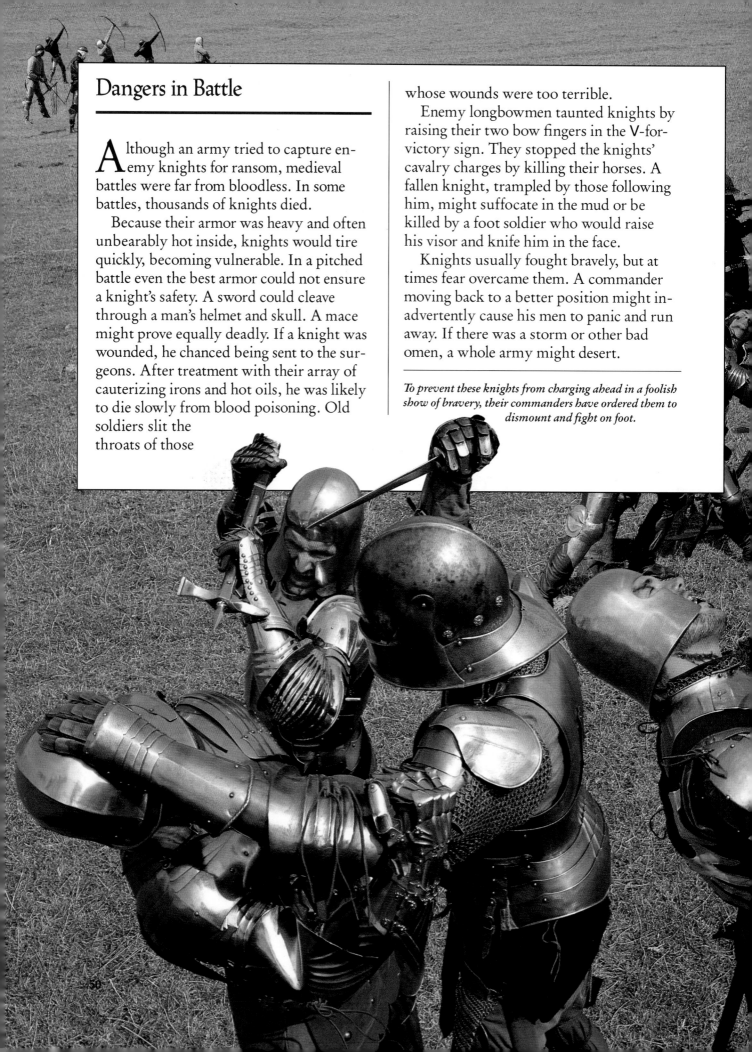

Dangers in Battle

Although an army tried to capture enemy knights for ransom, medieval battles were far from bloodless. In some battles, thousands of knights died.

Because their armor was heavy and often unbearably hot inside, knights would tire quickly, becoming vulnerable. In a pitched battle even the best armor could not ensure a knight's safety. A sword could cleave through a man's helmet and skull. A mace might prove equally deadly. If a knight was wounded, he chanced being sent to the surgeons. After treatment with their array of cauterizing irons and hot oils, he was likely to die slowly from blood poisoning. Old soldiers slit the throats of those whose wounds were too terrible.

Enemy longbowmen taunted knights by raising their two bow fingers in the V-for-victory sign. They stopped the knights' cavalry charges by killing their horses. A fallen knight, trampled by those following him, might suffocate in the mud or be killed by a foot soldier who would raise his visor and knife him in the face.

Knights usually fought bravely, but at times fear overcame them. A commander moving back to a better position might inadvertently cause his men to panic and run away. If there was a storm or other bad omen, a whole army might desert.

To prevent these knights from charging ahead in a foolish show of bravery, their commanders have ordered them to dismount and fight on foot.

50

The Chase

Between tournaments, knights loved to hunt. When Edward III of England invaded France in 1346, he brought 30 falconers and 60 pairs of hunting dogs. On his deathbed, Louis XI of France ordered his servants to release cats and mice in his room so he could indulge in the thrill of the chase.

Kings, barons, and knights all set aside large parts of their estates as game forests, or hunting grounds, and anyone caught trespassing was severely punished. In France, a nobleman hanged three young knights for poaching on his land. In England, the Bishop of Ely excommunicated a thief for stealing his favorite falcon.

The first specialized breeds of dog were developed for hunting: the lyam-hound (similar to a bloodhound), the gazehound (greyhound), and the alan (a wolfhound). Their large paved kennels were heated by fires and faced the sun. Servants fed the dogs and gave them fresh straw every day.

Knights hunted foxes, deer, hare, otters,

badgers, coneys (rabbits), wolves, and boars. They lured wolves into traps and beat them to death with sticks. Knights on horseback pursued wild boars, killing them with long, broad, sharp spears. The boar "is more formidable than an armed man," commented one medieval writer.

A knight goes hawking with his lady. The falconer, who has trained from childhood, carries the birds on a wooden frame. Each bird wears a hood and has jesses (leather straps) attached to its legs to stop it from escaping (inset). When prey is spotted, the falconer will select one of the birds, remove its hood, and release it.

The Tournament

In early tournaments, knights formed teams and tried to capture each other. This type of tournament was called a melee. A tournament was a way of training for war, but often the knights were so carried away that they refused to stop when ordered. Their squires joined in and the tournament became a real battle. Sometimes they fought *à outrance* — to the death.

When Edward I of England captured a French knight at a melee in 1274, the French counterattacked so furiously that the tournament became known as the Little War of Châlons.

After about 1400, however, tournaments changed. Pageantry and playacting increased. Stands, beautifully decorated with competitors' coats of arms, were erected for spectators. Knights organized events called *pas d'armes*, challenging other knights to joust with them. They pretended to defend a maiden in her castle or to rescue a lady from an evil giant. Tournaments became opportunities to show off and indulge in courtly love. By the late 15th century, tournaments were going out of fashion. At one *pas d'armes* in France, only one middle-aged German knight showed up.

In a joust two knights charge at each other. Each man tries to break his lance on his opponent's shield. They score points for the number of lances broken. Wearing heavy armor, including a helmet with a specially designed sight, or eye-slit, to protect them from accidental injury, they fight à plaisance, *for pleasure, with blunted or capped weapons. For additional safety, they joust "at the wooden fence barriers" with a between them.*

The Professional Soldier

The early knights were warriors, who were given land in return for their services to the king or emperor. As one generation succeeded another, however, knights became more involved in politics and less involved in war. Their estates required supervision, and soldiering was uncomfortable and dangerous. They preferred to enjoy the comforts of home—feasting, dancing, and playing dice and chess. Their sons studied law and got jobs in the government. When Edward I called out the English feudal army in 1277, only 377 knights reported for duty. Kings began to employ mercenaries, who signed a contract and were paid wages. In the English army in the 14th century, a knight received two shillings a day. In 1366 one shilling bought 6 pairs of gloves or 100 herrings.

These paid soldiers were reliable in battle, but when a war ended, they were left with nothing to do. During lulls in the fighting between the French and the English in the Hundred Years' War, huge gangs of mercenaries, called Free Companies, wandered around France robbing peasants and burning crops. They caused so much trouble that in 1439 Charles VII decided he would have to employ some of them full time. He hired one group as a permanent army and used it to destroy the others. The days of the feudal army were over; the age of the professional soldier had begun.

In Italy, these condottieri sell their services to the highest bidder. Towns pay the men to fight for them — then pay them to go away and pillage elsewhere.

The mercenaries are less interested in glory and chivalry than their predecessors were. They want to live to enjoy their earnings, so they devise safer tactics than those used by the earlier knights. Their aim is to win the battle with as few casualties as possible.

Gunpowder

Gunpowder, invented more than a thousand years ago in China, came to Europe in the Middle Ages. Europeans called it Chinese snow. At first, medieval writers thought that it was invented by evil magicians with the devil's help.

In about 1330 the Italians began to produce new weapons called thunder tubes (the word "cannon" comes from the Latin *canna*, meaning reed or tube). These thunder tubes, made of strips of metal welded together, used gunpowder to fire missiles. In France in 1375, 13 smiths, 3 forges, and 2,300 pounds (1,040 kilograms) of iron were needed to build one cannon. Although metal rings were welded around the barrels to stop the cannons from bursting, accidents were common; in 1460 King James II of Scotland was killed when a cannon exploded during a seige.

Large cannons made of wrought iron were called bombards. The English named their cannons after popular heroes such as Robin Hood. The French had one called The Greatest in the World.

Artillery design improved rapidly. At Bordeaux in 1420, an English cannon fired a stone cannonball weighing 784 pounds (356 kilograms). By the 16th century, bronze cannons were at last able to hurl a missile beyond the range of a longbow.

The cannon transformed siege warfare by reducing the length of a siege from over a year to a few months. Towns tried unsuccessfully to protect their walls by building mounds of earth in front of them. After 1450 every army employed cannoneers who built trenches around an enemy town or castle and directed the bombardment.

Cannoneers bombard the castle. Left, top to bottom: they pack gunpowder into the barrel, load the stone cannonball, then light a small charge of gunpowder above a hole in the barrel. A spark travels through the hole to ignite the main charge.

The New Knights

In the early Middle Ages, the knight was an almost invincible fighting machine. He was violent, sometimes cruel, and often uneducated. By the 16th century, however, many knights had ceased to be warriors. Their armor was a less reliable defense against injury and death than it had been. When knights fell from their horses they were now often killed. Cannons and handguns had replaced maces and mangonels as the supreme weapons.

In France, many merchants bought knighthoods because knights did not have to pay taxes. A middle-class French knight might put on his sword each morning and walk proudly past his warehouse. Tournaments, which had once been violent conflicts, now became ridiculous pageants. At the *pas d'armes* put on for the wedding of Charles the Bold in 1468, a female dwarf rode in on a mechanical lion and a life-size model whale sang and wiggled its tail. Nobles wore multicolored "slashed" clothes to copy Swiss foot soldiers, but they wore the clothes for dancing, not fighting.

Some knights still wore real armor and fought in real battles. They joined cavalry units and fought in disciplined groups called lances along with a number of hand-gunners and pikemen. These lances were used to attack the enemy or to chase enemy soldiers who ran away. If the attack failed, however, the riders no longer fought to the death. Instead, like the cavalry forces of later times, they fell back and regrouped behind the guns.

In 1605 the Spanish writer Cervantes tried to show that knights were not needed anymore. In his book *Don Quixote*, a tired old knight wanders about the countryside, charging at windmills that he believes are the enemy for the sake of a lady who is really just a peasant girl. His "silly ideals of knight errantry" make him look foolish, and his actions make the ideals look foolish as well.

The pikemen are grouped in a pointed hedgehog formation, with the bravest soldiers in front. Behind the pikes the handgunners reload. In the distance the knights prepare to charge, but by the 16th century a well-ordered unit of pikemen is virtually invulnerable to a cavalry charge.

How Do We Know?

We can gather a great deal of evidence about the knights and their world through the writing, art, and objects of the Middle Ages that have survived the centuries. The difficulty for the historian is to decide what to believe and how to understand the different sources.

LITERARY SOURCES FROM THE MIDDLE AGES

Many books were written about knighthood and chivalry in the Middle Ages themselves, including *The Art of Courtly Love* (1186) by Andreas Capellanus, *The Book of the Ordre of Chyvalrie* (1265) by Raimon Llull, and *Le Jouvencel* (1462–67) by Jean de Bueil. These books are essentially manuals, primarily designed to describe how a knight ought to behave.

Other writers described the events of the time. One of the most reliable and informative chroniclers was a Frenchman called Jean Froissart (1337–1410), who wrote a history of the Hundred Years' War. His account contains many fascinating stories about knights, some of which appear in this book.

Reading and writing were taught mainly in the monasteries during the Middle Ages, so many writers of the time were churchmen and churchwomen — the last name Capellanus, for example, means chaplain. Many of these writers disliked the warlike knights or sought to control their behavior, so they included unpleasant gossip, some of it completely made up, in their accounts of the knights' exploits. Reading many of the documents written during this period, one

might think that in the Middle Ages the Church was all-powerful, the women were weak, and all the knights were brutal. We know that this is not the whole story.

Other kinds of documents have survived from the Middle Ages. Historians can read thousands of royal writs (written orders), notations of financial transactions, and records of court cases. Many nobles — the Paston family in England, for instance —

kept records of their estates and saved much of their correspondence. These records often provide fascinating details of everyday life.

To add to this knowledge, we can read wonderful stories such as the medieval romances and the *chansons de geste*, Chaucer's *Canterbury Tales*, and Cervantes's *Don Quixote*. Literature can be helpful because it contains details of real life, though it doesn't precisely reflect life as it was actually lived. The stories people tell reveal much about their attitudes, wishes, and beliefs.

OTHER SOURCES

There are more ways to find out about the knights than simply by reading about them. Some of the objects they owned can still be found, and many of the castles they lived in still exist and welcome visitors. Today, we can peer through an arrow slit or climb down into an oubliette (the dungeon where prisoners were thrown and forgotten), sit on a knight's chair, handle his weapons, or wear his armor.

We can also look at tapestries made by the knights' wives or paintings made by medieval artists. The tapestries show knights in battle and out hunting. The

paintings of the time usually illustrate Bible stories, but the artists show the biblical characters in medieval clothes and armor and depict them living in medieval towns, providing a glimpse into medieval life.

INTO MODERN TIMES

After Cervantes, chivalry was forgotten until the 19th century, when Sir Walter Scott wrote his great romantic novel, *Ivanhoe* (1819). For a while, knights and chivalry came back into fashion. In 1839 the Earl of Eglington, a rich young English lord, held a full-scale tournament complete with lavish pavilions, horses, and costumes.

Early in the 20th century, Hollywood producers discovered the Middle Ages, and the tales of the knights in armor were retold on film. Although we know that the Middle Ages weren't exactly like the stories that people told then or now, the exciting adventures of the knights and the pageantry of the tournaments continue to capture the imagination.

Index

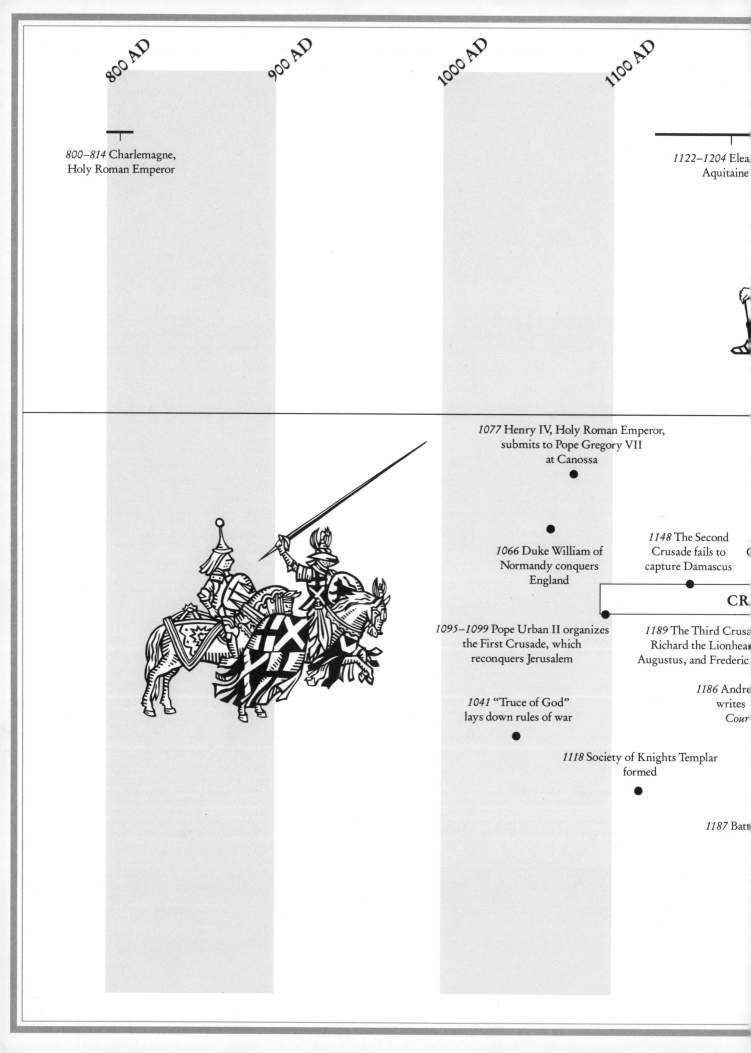

800 AD

900 AD

1000 AD

1100 AD

800–814 Charlemagne,
Holy Roman Emperor

1122–1204 Elea
Aquitaine

1077 Henry IV, Holy Roman Emperor,
submits to Pope Gregory VII
at Canossa

1066 Duke William of
Normandy conquers
England

1148 The Second
Crusade fails to
capture Damascus

CR

1095–1099 Pope Urban II organizes
the First Crusade, which
reconquers Jerusalem

1189 The Third Crusa
Richard the Lionhea
Augustus, and Frederic

1186 Andre
writes
Cour

1041 "Truce of God"
lays down rules of war

1118 Society of Knights Templar
formed

1187 Batt